Sleeping Under Clouds

❧

Sue Wallace-Shaddad

and

Sula Rubens R.W.S.

CLAYHANGER PRESS | NEWCASTLE-UNDER-LYME

First Printing, 2023

Published by Clayhanger Press
Newcastle under Lyme
Staffordshire
www.clayhangerpress.co.uk

ISBN-978-1-7391770-2-7

Sleeping Under Clouds

Contents

This Map   8

Traces   9

Keeping Going   10

History Lesson   11

Background Music   12

On the Road   13

Questions   14

Held   16

Mother and Child   18

Together   20

In the Air   22

Watch Out   24

Umbrella   26

Two   28

Framed   30

Weighing Up the Options   32

On the Sofa   34

Stolen Moment   36

Kin   38

Rising   40

Tipping Point   42

What's in a Name?   44

Interdependent   46

Grounded   48

Flight   50

Passage   52

List of paintings by Sula Rubens, R.W.S.   54

Acknowledgements   55

Biographies   56

In 2017 Sula Rubens began her series entitled *Kin* which has people as its primary focus. Although there is no direct reference in the work to the displacement and suffering of refugees, some of the people portrayed are displaced, struggling to survive and protect their kin. They are transient figures moving through spaces she creates for them on canvas, maps or book pages. She portrays them outside, vulnerable to the sea and the sky and sometimes with mountains in the distance, carrying a sense of the faraway lands from which they might have travelled.

Sue Wallace-Shaddad's 'Kin' poems respond to specific images in the *Kin* series and in 'Maps' she explores the feelings evoked by an overview of the totality of Sula's exploration of the reality of being dispossessed of place and security. The poems explore the hinterland of emotions embedded in the daily survival of people, particularly children, on the move. Themes which emerge include kinship, journeying, nurture, memories of the past, uncertainty about the future and the interdependency of shared existence.

For all the children who have no choice

MAPS

This Map

has many paths
each route another choice

an atlas of possibilities
daunting in its scope

roads stretch out
touching the distance

traced precisely
like filigree lace

spun cobwebs
a silken invitation

to fall between the lines
end up somewhere else

Traces

Each line marks a border
drawn by the suffering
of humankind, a map

where rivers, blue-veined,
crisscross the skin
of an ancient hand,

delicate, paper-thin.
People pass *so lightly here.*
Curly heads droop, limbs tire.

They seek a porous fence,
a welcoming world
where they can rest,

free of the cold, the wet,
where children may sleep
under roofs not clouds.

Keeping Going

I've never met these children
on the move but their footsteps
carry me into their world,
each border that they cross,
one step nearer to their goal,
safety, a chance for better lives.

I can never hope to understand
the language of their pain or see
the images that fill their sleep
at night. They have to keep going,
struggle past those memories which
cannot be erased from their minds.

History Lesson

Each map serves a purpose,
filling the canvas with hope,
foreign-sounding names
difficult to pronounce.

Places with their own history
of war and suffering, floods
and drought. Places haunted
by shifting patterns of people

seeking shelter, seeking peace.
Sometimes the lines are faint,
sometimes coloured bold.
They serve to remind me

places reinvent themselves,
new lives building on the old.

Background Music

Brushstrokes create the scene
before my eyes, the backstory,
a narrative of disrupted lives.

If music were added, there'd be
a powerful score, punctuated
by moments of calm. The strings

would stretch their wings, drums
beat to the incessant pad of steps.
There'd be an orchestra of sound,

the brass strident in their demands,
the clash of cymbals accompanied
by a liquid run of piano notes.

A percussion of children
would enliven the road
with a ting-ting of triangles,

tambourines in small hands,
bright brittleness of a xylophone,
the ringing of some bells.

I also hear howling wind, slash
of rain, breath of bodies huddled
for warmth when the sea is done.

On the Road

The nanny grubs around the tent
for scraps of grass to eat,

her milk warm and white,
a source of sustenance

in a barren landscape
where little is sure.

Windblown sand and flies
crowd around her face.

She remains close, tethered.
She has no name.

Soon they will pack and leave,
shifting like desert dunes.

The journeying will be long.
She will not die where she was born.

Questions

If I had to walk that far
I'd get blisters on my feet,
my skin would crack, hair
straggle down my back.
I'd complain of my lot, find it
hard to keep my spirits up.

I wouldn't have the memories
these children have buried
deep. I haven't faced
the destruction of my home,
lived the journey across maps
that makes them who they are.

If I were given no choice,
caught in the thread of fate,
how would I react? Walking
step by slow step, would I bond
with others by my side
yet hold my identity fast?

KIN

Held

'Protecting, till the danger past, with human love'
from 'Prayer for my Son' by WB Yeats

The lines are clean, strokes bold.
Drawn to each other, they rest,

the child nestling into her body,
his shoulder rounded. He stares

back into the blue. Her hand,
protective, holds him still.

There's solidity in the gesture,
a certainty which states

no-one may come between.
She remembers how it felt

to hold him, newly born,
the warmth of his tiny body

milk-soft against her breast.
She has no choice; she knows

she must keep him safe.
She sees what he cannot.

Self Portrait "Protecting, till the danger past, with human love". [Oil on canvas, 72 x 62 cm]

Mother and Child

A quiet moment
of give and take

hand outstretched
thumb caressing lip

an answering smile
a softened gaze

skin touching skin
a whispered kiss

for now, at least,
they own this world

Madonna and Child. [Watercolour on paper (map), 25.4 x 19 cm]

Together

These children come as a package,
none can be left behind. Kith or kin,
they're kept close, shouldered high,
hands held, or walking alongside.

If people still sent letters,
postage stamps would show
a pictorial record of every
country that they cross.

Each step on their journey
brings them nearer to the moment
of delivery, when they will
remember all they have lost.

Kin Study – Family. [Watercolour on paper (map), 24 x 19 cm]

In the Air

Headed firmly in the air,
the football greets the sky,
hanging like a half moon.

A memory of days at home
kicking around with friends,
bare feet in the dust, before

their world broke apart,
the pitch blown up,
their games disrupted.

Now they find a spot
wherever they can, join
together to field a team,

each game a chance
to laugh, to meet
on common ground.

Three Boys with Football. [Oil on canvas, 76 x 91 cm]

Watch Out

there's a leopard behind you,
all yellow with brown spots,
balancing on the washing line!

He could tiptoe along, climb
down with animal ease.
Always on the lookout,

he's spied the fluffy lamb
held in your arms. He fancies
a taste of fresh meat,

but you are not afraid
of some phantom in the wind.
You hold a beating heart.

Kin Study – Young Boy holding a Lamb. [Watercolour on paper (map), 19 x 24 cm]

Umbrella

A colourful semaphore of sorts,
the washing billows on the line.

The umbrella, a little out of place
with its flowery border on blue,

might give shelter from the sun
though the season looks cool.

The boy owns it with pride,
a distinctive accessory to tote.

He prefers to be observer
and watch the others play.

Rain is nowhere in sight.
Dry dust will soon be kicked up

by bike, football, games of chase,
just add two curious kids to the mix.

Three Boys and Two Young Goats. [Watercolour and acrylic on paper, 38 x 47 cm]

Two

The children are purposeful
holding the umbrella together,

their own private space.
It might be raining

in their greyed-out world
but the yellow suggests

the sun may shine; flowers
spring up along the edges.

One older than the other,
they share the same view.

Kin Study – Two Children with Umbrella. [Watercolour on paper (book page), 18.5 x 24.5cm]

Framed

The boy's hands embrace
the mackerel-striped tabby,
feel his beating heart.

Both look at us with steady gaze
as if staring into a mirror, image
fixed in the doorway.

Unusually still for a cat, fur soft,
he's named after an Arab city
known for fashioning silk cloth.

Sharp-eared, he listens out
for sounds, his whiskers alert,
ready to sense possible prey.

How long before he struggles
to free himself from this frame?
Will he be wild again?

Boy holding his Cat (Fadi and Aleppo). [Watercolour and acrylic on paper, 49 x 36 cm]

Weighing Up the Options

The tyres' tread appears good,
several hundred miles to go.
Ready to be rolled with ease.

A useful find. The children
dream of playing games,
of lodging them in the sand

then weaving in and out
or straddling the tops,
testing their imagination.

They don't have much
to brighten their days, no
expensive gift-wrapped toys.

They even hope to cajole
grown-ups to build a swing
for their childish pleasure.

Four Children with Tyres. [Oil on canvas, 71 x 107 cm]

On the Sofa

This sofa is weary, its cushions
no longer plump, the cream piping's limp.

How many children have pummelled the stuffing,
jumped, pillow-fought, feathers flying?

Now stranded on a beach, exposed, alone,
it's uncertain who might grace its faded dignity.

A group of children wander up, arrange themselves,
chat as if waiting to be photographed.

Kin – Five Children and Sofa in a Landscape. [Oil on canvas, 71 x 127 cm]

Stolen Moment

A calming hand, a quiet word
and the mare stays close.

Cheek to cheek, the girl softens
in the warmth of their embrace.

Whatever the distance travelled,
whatever the sights they've seen,

they picture lush meadows,
streams, forget those stony paths,

the hardship mixed with hope,
the unforgiving beat of sun and rain.

A moment of rest, not knowing
when the next may come.

Mountain Girl with Horse. [Ink, watercolour & acrylic on paper, 36.5 x 37 cm]

Kin

Mountains and olive trees
encircle the young goatherds,
pretty in their cotton dresses.

The elder girl, a mother-figure,
comfortable in her skin,
clasps the wrist of her sister,

looking after her own, just as
the goat tends to her kids,
a bell to ward off wolves.

Kin – Three Goats and Two Girls. [Oil on canvas, 130 x 107 cm]

Rising

Head against cheek,
arms holding tight,

they rise from the water
like disembodied ghosts.

No words to explain
from where they have come.

The sea is a foreign place.
Not all will escape.

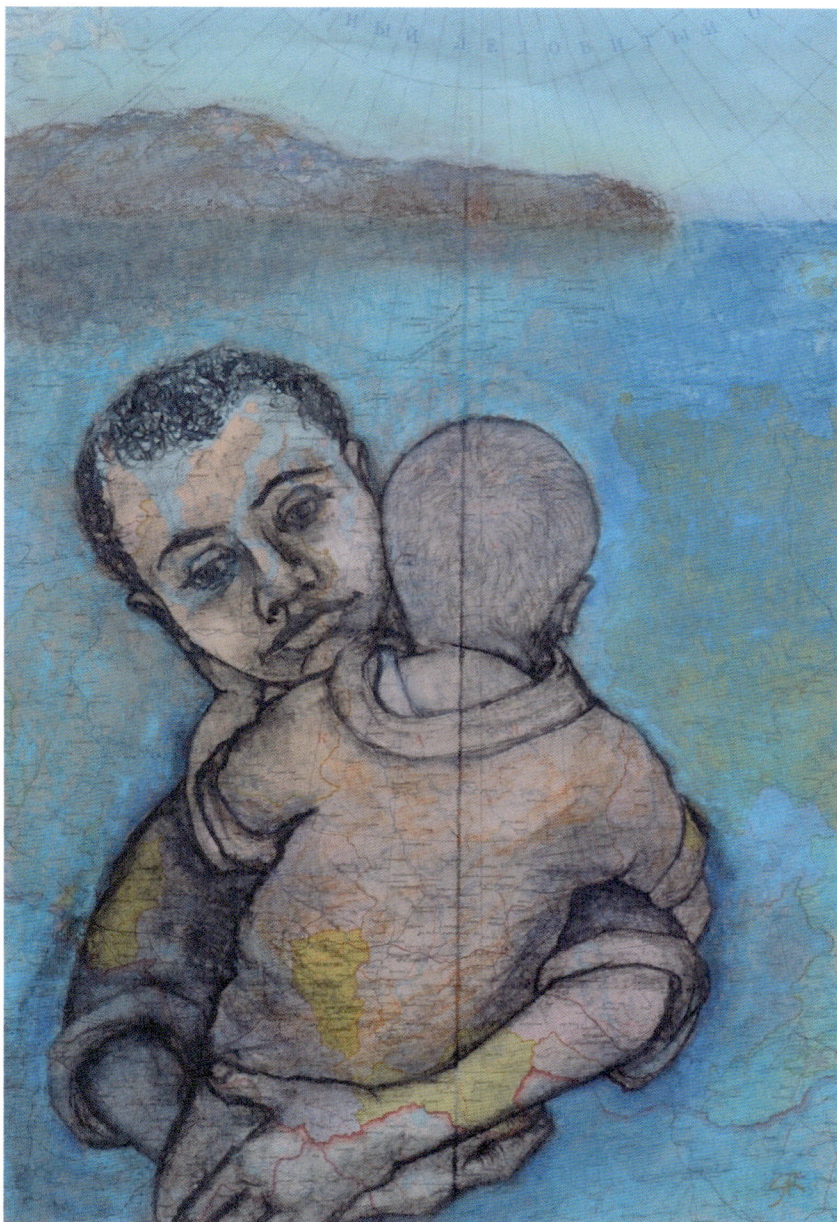

Kin – Boy carrying Young Child. [Charcoal, watercolour & pigment on paper (map), 61 x 42 cm]

Tipping Point

He might suddenly dive
into the marbled depths
mapped in front of him.

Tilting his curved body
like a moon on its axis,
he calls out to the tides.

Suspended, he listens
to the siren sea, so close
yet so full of mystery.

He feels the play of sunlight
and imagines floating free,
water caressing his skin.

Boy at Water's Edge. [Acrylic on antique marbled book cover, 24 x 17 cm]

What's in a Name?

His name, Fadi, means 'saviour',
a strong name to give to a child.
Who knows what he may face?

His cat, Aleppo, tells of a city
left behind, its streets empty,
homes ground to dust.

They save each other, boy and cat,
feeling the comfort of connection:
a laugh, a purr, a stroke of luck.

They have the same outlook,
they fend for themselves.
You can see it in their eyes.

Fadi holding his cat Aleppo. [Ink, watercolour & pastel on paper, 40 x 37 cm]

Interdependent

(triptych)

I.

The boys stand, backs
to the sea, a loose rope
linking them to the heifer.

She shares the same
ground, the same dust,
the same sparse grass.

They've already learnt
that animals matter,
football has to wait.

II.

Along the same wall
bordering the sea, a girl
looks after a donkey.

He carries her weight,
accompanies her
on daily tasks,

his makeshift bridle
waiting for a tug,
a flick of her wrist.

III.

Nearby, a gaggle of geese
face every which way.
No sense of direction.

Red-cheeked, a boy holds
tight to a white-feathered
bird, soon to be plucked

or just returned to the fold.
His job, to keep them in order,
no chance of keeping them quiet.

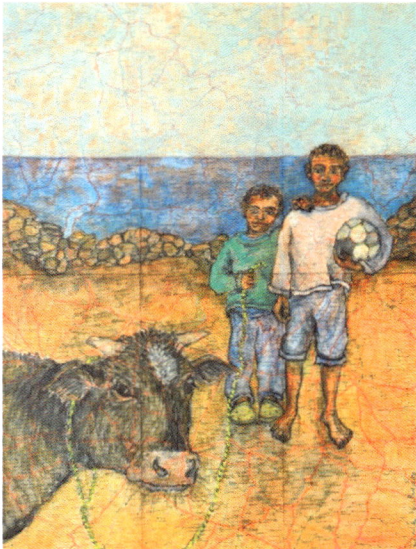

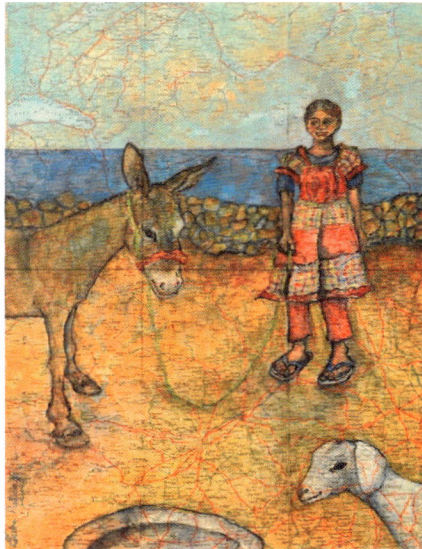

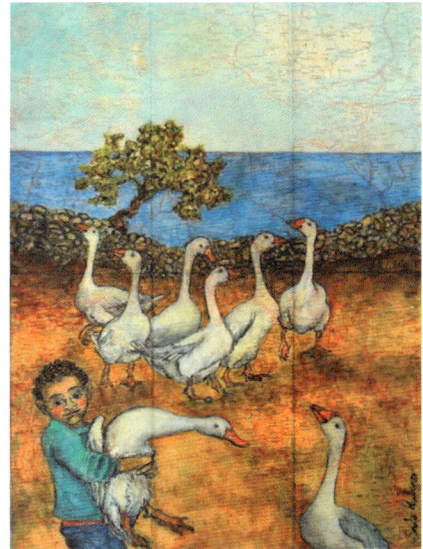

Kin Triptych – Two Boys with Cow and Football. [Watercolour on paper (map), 53 x 37 cm]
Kin Triptych – Girl with Donkey and a Young Goat. [Watercolour on paper (map) 53 x 37 cm]
Kin Triptych – Boy with Geese. [Watercolour on paper (map) 53 x 37 cm]

Grounded

These geese, painted on a map,
seem at ease, but look north
as if missing their ancestral home.

They parade up and down
with conversational honking,
friendly, insistent, hard to ignore.

Plump, waddling on webbed feet,
will they be kept until old age?
They're bound to the land

unlike pink-footed cousins
traversing the night sky in skeins,
wings measuring the dark.

Two Geese, Study. [Watercolour on paper (map) 21 x 13.5 cm]

Flight

They travel with the wind,
wings outstretched, tip to tip,
whole families on the move,

rivers and coastlines beneath.
The land holds no borders
for them, maps have no use.

They follow their instincts,
that inner compass set
to guide them surely home.

Above our heads, the song
of their shadows announces
their passage through our lives.

Shore Flight – Migration. [Watercolour & pastel on paper (map) 19 x 26 cm]

Passage

The ground is hard, even stony
but a tired head needs a place to rest.
Tucked up under a tasselled rug,
the child holds on to a ragged bear,
a small comfort by his side.

Tomorrow they'll pack up,
follow the edge of fields,
looking out for food to forage.
They'll hope for dull weather,
neither rain nor blazing sun.

Each footstep marks the distance
travelled, shoes wearing thin.
Gripped by a steady hand or carried
shoulder-high, the child holds tight
till night falls and he sleeps again.

Kin Study – Sleeping Child in a Landscape. [Watercolour on paper (map) 26 x 38 cm]

List of paintings by Sula Rubens, R.W.S.

Self Portrait "Protecting, till the danger past, with human love". [Oil on canvas, 72 x 62 cm]................17
Madonna and Child. [Watercolour on paper (map), 25.4 x 19 cm].....................19
Kin Study – Family. [Watercolour on paper (map), 24 x 19 cm]...........................21
Three Boys with Football. [Oil on canvas, 76 x 91 cm]..23
Kin Study – Young Boy holding a Lamb. [Watercolour on paper (map), 19 x 24 cm]........25
Three Boys and Two Young Goats. [Watercolour and acrylic on paper, 38 x 47 cm]........27
Kin Study – Two Children with Umbrella. [Watercolour on paper (book page), 18.5 x 24.5cm]..........29
Boy holding his Cat (Fadi and Aleppo). [Watercolour and acrylic on paper, 49 x 36 cm]........31
Four Children with Tyres. [Oil on canvas, 71 x 107 cm].......................................33
Kin – Five Children and Sofa in a Landscape. [Oil on canvas, 71 x 127 cm].....................35
Mountain Girl with Horse. [Ink, watercolour & acrylic on paper, 36.5 x 37 cm].................37
Kin – Three Goats and Two Girls. [Oil on canvas, 130 x 107 cm] 39
Kin – Boy carrying Young Child. [Charcoal, watercolour & pigment on paper (map), 61 x 42 cm 41
Boy at Water's Edge. [Acrylic on antique marbled book cover, 24 x 17 cm]....................43
Fadi holding his cat Aleppo. [Ink, watercolour & pastel on paper, 40 x 37 cm] 45
Kin Triptych – Two Boys with Cow and Football. [Watercolour on paper (map), 53 x 37 cm] 47
Kin Triptych – Girl with Donkey and a Young Goat. [Watercolour on paper (map) 53 x 37 cm]..........47
Kin Triptych – Boy with Geese. [Watercolour on paper (map) 53 x 37 cm]....................47
Two Geese, Study. [Watercolour on paper (map) 21 x 13.5 cm]..............................49
Shore Flight – Migration. [Watercolour & pastel on paper (map) 19 x 26 cm]........................51
Kin Study – Sleeping Child in a Landscape. [Watercolour on paper (map) 26 x 38 cm] 53

Acknowledgements

'Watch Out' was published by *Second Light Publications*, ARTEMIS poetry issue 25, November 2020.

'Umbrella' was published by *Finished Creatures*, Issue 7, March 2023.

'Traces' was published under the *Personal History of Home Project* supported by TORCH (The Oxford Research Centre in the Humanities, University of Oxford) October 2022.   https://www.torch.ac.uk/personal-history-home

'so lightly here', quoted in 'Traces', comes from Leonard Cohen's lyrics in *Boogie Street* which Sula Rubens highlighted as important to her thinking.

Photography of artworks by Jon Wilson and Jake Fuller.

We would like to thank Roger Bloor, Clayhanger Press, for his care and attention to the layout and quality of images in this publication.

Finally, we would like to recognize the power of collaboration across genres and the inspiration that each of us has brought to the table in creating this publication.

Biographies

Sula Rubens R.W.S. studied at Central/St. Martin's School of Art (BA Hons Fine Art), where she was influenced by working practices and theories of artist/tutors – Tricia Gillman, Alan Reynolds, Norman Ackroyd, Anthony Whishaw and Cecil Collins. Since graduating in 1989, she has practised as a painter and printmaker. She has lived, worked and exhibited in many cities including Amsterdam in Holland, Gdansk in Poland, St. Petersburg in Russia as well as the rural landscapes of France, Spain, Greece and Ireland. Often travelling to paint, Sula has immersed herself in various landscapes, buildings and their people. She has collaborated with artists, poets and musicians nationally and internationally.

Her work is represented in public and private collections in this country and abroad, including The Royal Watercolour Society Diploma Collection, Leicestershire Collection for Schools and Colleges and the Town Council of Amsterdam. Residencies include the Westerkerk in Amsterdam, the South Lookout Tower on Aldeburgh beach and Potton Hall Recording Studio in Suffolk. In 2014 she was appointed as the first Artist in Residence at The Michaelhouse in Cambridge.

In 2019 she was elected by the Royal Watercolour Society to become an Associate Member. In 2022 she was honoured with full membership.

Sue Wallace-Shaddad has an MA in Writing Poetry from Newcastle University with the Poetry School London. Her pamphlet *'A City Waking Up'* was published by Dempsey and Windle, October 2020. Sue was highly commended in the Plough Poetry Prize 2021 and has had several pamphlets recently shortlisted or longlisted by Maytree Press. Her poems have featured in *London Grip, Artemis, The Ekphrastic Review, The High Window, Fenland Poetry Journal, Ink, Sweat & Tears, Poetry Scotland, Poetry Space, Finished Creatures* among others and in various anthologies. Sue writes regular poetry reviews for *Sphinx Review, London Grip* and *The Alchemy Spoon*. Since her retirement in 2014 from a long career with the British Council, she has been Secretary of Suffolk Poetry Society and helps run the Society's annual festival and other events. Sue runs a regular café evening in Ipswich with invited poets. She is digital writer-in-residence for the Charles Causley Trust's Literary Blog *The Maker*.
https://suewallaceshaddad.wordpress.com

Typeset in Book Antiqua

Cover Design by Clayhanger Press

The cover image is *Kin – Boy carrying Young Child.* © Sula Rubens R.W.S.
Typesetting and Design Roger Bloor

Copy Editor Sara Levy

www.clayhangerpress.co.uk

Clayhanger Press

Printed in Great Britain
by Amazon